The Secret Grove

by Barbara Cohen

illustrated by
Michael J. Deraney

HARCOURT BRACE & COMPANY
Orlando Atlanta Austin Boston San Francisco Chicago Dallas New York
Toronto London

This edition is published by special arrangement with McIntosh and Otis, Inc. and Union of American Hebrew Congregation.

Grateful acknowledgment is made to McIntosh and Otis, Inc. and Union of American Hebrew Congregation for permission to reprint *The Secret Grove* by Barbara Cohen, illustrated by Michael J. Deraney. Text copyright © 1985 by Barbara Cohen; illustrations copyright © 1985 by Michael J. Deraney. Published by Union of American Hebrew Congregation.

Printed in the United States of America

ISBN 0-15-302225-6

2 3 4 5 6 7 8 9 10   011   97 96 95 94 93

With grateful appreciation
to Rabbi Benjamin A. Kamin
for sharing an incident
from his childhood
which inspired this book.
                    BC

For my brother and sister-in-law,
David and Sue.
                    MJD

I have a secret. I've had it for years now—since I was ten.

In those days, I lived in a village called Kfar-Saba, near the Yarkon River. On the other side of the road was a village called Qalqilya. No one ever went from Kfar-Saba to Qalqilya. No one ever went from Qalqilya to Kfar-Saba. We in Kfar-Saba were Jews, Israelis. They in Qalqilya were Arabs, Jordanians.

I listened to the radio. I heard grown-ups talk.

Arab terrorists attacked Israeli schools and markets.

The Israeli Air Force raided Jordan and Lebanon.

When I was five, most men in Kfar-Saba had gone

down into the Sinai to fight the Egyptians. But not my father. He had only one arm. He'd lost the other one battling Arabs in Israel's War of Independence.

Nearly every family in our village had a photograph set out on a table of an uncle or a cousin, a son or a brother, who'd been killed in one of the wars.

But I didn't worry much about war. I worried more about being short for my age and so clumsy that I tended to fall over my own feet.

Around Kfar-Saba, fields and orchards stretched

thick and green. Beyond them lay the mountains, rocky and bare against the blazing blue of the sky. In late fall and winter the rains came; the rest of the year the sun shone. I swam and hiked. I played soccer with my friends, when they let me.

Sometimes we went to the movies. I read books. At night I watched programs on television. And naturally I went to school.

I liked the teacher we had in fifth grade. With her we could talk about lots of things besides what was in our

texts. When we read the Ten Commandments in the Bible, we talked for a long time about each one of them. We talked for half an hour about "Thou shalt not steal."

"It's wrong to steal from anyone," Anat said. "But it's worse to steal from your mother."

"No one would steal from his mother!" Ari said. "It's not possible."

"It *is* hard to believe," the teacher said. Up and down the rows, heads nodded in agreement.

Anat stood up, her hands on her hips. "It's possible," she insisted. "I knew this girl once who took money right out of her mother's purse."

"Oh, I don't believe it," Dan said. "No one would steal from his mother."

"No one we know," Tamar said.

"Except maybe an Arab," Boaz suggested.

"Well, maybe an Arab would," Ari agreed.

The teacher shrugged. "Perhaps you're right," she said.

We talked a little more, but then it was time to go home. After lunch, Ari stopped at my house. "Come on, Beni," he said, "bring your ball and we'll play soccer in the schoolyard." My ball had the most life. It was new, a birthday present.

A whole bunch of guys were waiting for us behind the school. Ari was the captain of one team; Dan was the captain of the other. They tossed a coin to see who would pick first. Dan won. "I pick Boaz," he said. Boaz walked over and stood behind Dan.

It was Ari's turn, my friend Ari. "I pick Menny," he said.

"Shmuel," Dan said.

Ari's eyes narrowed as he glanced quickly at each one of us. For a second he focused on me, and my heart rose into my throat. "Ishai," he said.

I didn't even hear the next names that were called. I

knew they weren't mine. I always got picked last, each
captain hoping until the end that the other team would
be stuck with me. Today wasn't going to be any differ-
ent.

A thought bubbled to the top of my brain. If it
weren't for my ball, they wouldn't even have asked me
to play. A great rush of anger boiled through me. Suddenly I knew I wasn't going to stand there in the dust
waiting once more to be the schlemiel who's left over. I
picked up my feet and started to run.

"Hey, Beni, where're you going?" Ari called.

I didn't even turn around. I didn't even answer him. I

just kept running. I ran until I couldn't hear the sound of their voices any more. I ran until I had left the streets and houses of the town behind me. Then I stopped running. I was breathing in shallow gulps that sounded like sobs.

I left the road and cut through the fields, following a kind of dim, overgrown track. I didn't know where I was going; I only knew that I wanted to put as much distance between myself and the Kfar-Saba schoolyard as I could. But, now that I was traveling more slowly, I looked up. In the distance I could see the blue dome of a mosque mounding gently above the flat-roofed houses of Qalqilya. Perhaps long ago the path I was on had been a road running between the two towns.

I knew I mustn't go any further. My mother had warned me to stay far away from the barbed-wire fence which in those days marked the Israel-Jordan border. The enemies of the Jews, she said, were everywhere—but especially there.

Along the track bloomed a little orange grove. I'd never seen it before; I didn't know who it belonged to. I was hot and thirsty and tired. I picked a fat ripe orange from a branch that hung low across the path and sat down under the tree to eat it.

And then, coming along the path in the other direction, I saw a boy. On his head he wore a kaffiyeh. I knew he was an Arab.

He saw me at the same moment that I saw him. On my head I wore a small crocheted skullcap, a kipah. He knew me for a Jew.

I jumped to my feet. What should I do? Run back to

Kfar-Saba as fast as my legs could carry me? There might be others behind him. They might throw stones at me. They might beat me up. They could even kill me.

The boy stood still, about ten meters away from me, staring with wide, dark eyes. He was no taller than I, and no heavier. Like me, he wore khaki shorts and a dirty white tee shirt.

No others followed him up the path. I didn't move. He didn't move. We stood there, eyeing each other, like two dogs meeting for the first time.

"Are these your orange trees?" I called. I didn't want him to think *I* was a thief. And then I wondered if he could understand what I was saying.

He shook his head. So he did understand. "Kfar-Saba?" He stepped toward me.

I nodded. I still felt nervous, but now more from excitement than fear. "Qalqilya?" I returned.

"Yes," he said. "My name is Ahmed." He spoke in hesitant English.

"I'm Beni," I replied, also in English. "I'm ten."

"I'm nine and a half. I'll be ten in February." By this time we were standing next to each other.

"I'm small for my age," I admitted.

He seemed confused. Using my hands as I spoke, I explained. "I am ten. Everyone else who is ten is bigger."

He smiled. "I too am not enough big," he said. "I will grow. You will grow."

I couldn't speak any Arabic, but he spoke a few words of Hebrew and enough English so that we could manage a conversation. We sat under the tree, eating oranges and talking. He liked to watch soccer on the television, but he liked to play it better. His father owned a garage and was the headman in the village. He had six brothers and three sisters. Four of the children were younger than he was; five were older. His mother and father believed in education. All the children in the family had to finish school, even the girls.

I told him about my three sisters, and my father, who had only one arm and taught mathematics, and my mother, who had two and drove a tractor. I even told him about my new soccer ball, and how I got picked last for the team anyway.

The shadows cast by the orange trees grew longer, and the evening wind came up. "I think I have to go," Ahmed said.

I glanced upwards and saw the sun close to the horizon. "Me too," I said. "They'll wonder what happened to me if I don't get home for supper."

"Will you come back?" Ahmed asked.

I ran my fingers through my hair before I answered. "Yes," I said. "I'll come back." The next day, Wednesday, I was going to Tel Aviv with my mother and father. "I'll come on Thursday, the same time, after school."

But, on Thursday, it rained. It was early in the season for rain, but it was good for the winter wheat and no one in Kfar-Saba was sorry to see it, except me. After lunch, I put on a jacket and cap and started for the door.

"Where're you going?" my mother asked me.

"For a walk," I said. I couldn't lie and tell her I was running next door to Ari's house. I'd come home soaked, and she'd know I'd been outside longer than two minutes. But I couldn't tell her the truth either.

"In the rain? Are you crazy?"

"It's not raining so hard."

"It's pouring, and you just got over a cold. Stay in and do your homework. Then you can read one of the books Aba brought home for you, or play with your sisters."

"I don't want to play with my sisters."

"Then don't. But you're not going out. You'll end up with pneumonia again, like you had last year. You stay right here and do your homework."

It rained on and off for three days. It was Sunday before I could return to the little grove. Every time a breeze shook the branches of the orange trees, the leaves showered water onto the damp earth. There wasn't another human being in sight.

I hadn't really expected to find him there again. Still, I waited. For five minutes, for ten, for fifteen. For half an hour. And then, just as I had made up my mind to leave, he came into view over the rise in the muddy track, pushing a rusty bicycle with one hand and carrying a book in the other.

"Ahmed!" I called.

"Beni!" he returned.

"I'm sorry I wasn't here on Thursday. My mother wouldn't let me out in the rain."

"Rain so early. Everyone's happy. It's a good sign."

We talked a little about weather and crops, like two grown-ups. Then we talked about school, our friends, and games. "How do you say soccer in Arabic?" I asked.

"*Layba el-toba.* The game of football."

"In Hebrew it's *kadur regel*," I offered. I pointed to his bike. "How do you say that in Arabic?"

"*Darraja,*" he said. He pointed to my sneakers. He was wearing sandals. "How do you say them in Hebrew?"

"*Na'alai tennis.*"

He laughed. "We do the same thing. We take the Arabic word for shoe and put the English word after it. *Heetha tennis* we say."

In half an hour we exchanged twenty-five or thirty words, rushing to get in as many as we could. We had so little time. I said it first. "You know, I have to go."

He nodded. "But, before, I must show you something." He opened the book he'd brought with him. "This is my history book," he said. "From school." Of course, I couldn't read the words, but I understood the picture he was pointing at. It was a cartoon of an Israeli soldier. His face was uglier than Frankenstein's, but you knew he was supposed to be Jewish because of the big six-pointed star on his helmet. He held a gun with a bayonet, and he was pointing it at an Arab woman clutching a baby to her breast.

"That's not true," I said. "That picture is not true. It's a terrible lie."

He nodded slowly.

I didn't ask him if he would steal money from his mother. I knew such a question would make him as angry as the picture had made me.

And he didn't ask me if I would come again. He had to sneak under a barbed-wire fence. I had to escape my sharp-eyed mother. It was too difficult. We both knew that.

One huge, bright orange hung within reach of our hands. I plucked it off the tree. "One for the road," I said. I peeled it and held half of it out to him. We sucked the juice from the flesh, then chewed and swallowed it, spitting the pits on the ground.

Suddenly he squatted and began gathering the pits.
"What are you doing, Ahmed?" I asked.

"Let's plant them," he said.

"Yes, let's." I knelt too and retrieved as many as I
could. "Let's take five big ones and plant them together.
Maybe one will take and grow."

With sticks we scraped out a little hole in the mud.
We dropped in five healthy looking pits. We covered
them with dirt.

We stood up. I wiped my hand on my shorts and held it out to him. "*Salaam aleiqem*, Ahmed," I said. They were the only Arabic words I'd known before that day.

He shook it. "*Shalom*, Beni," he replied.

We moved off down the track, in opposite directions.

Suddenly, I turned. He had turned, too. We lifted our arms and waved to each other. Then once again we each went on our way.

I never saw him again.

Eventually, I grew tall enough and strong enough, just as he had said I would. In the twenty years since our meeting, there've been three wars between the Arabs and the Israelis. I've fought in two of them.

Has he?

I don't live in Kfar-Saba anymore. But I go back there sometimes to visit my mother and father. When I can, I take a walk outside of the town.

The orange tree we planted still grows in the little grove between Kfar-Saba and Qalqilya. Its branches are heavy with fruit. Always I pick one of the oranges and eat it. Its juice is the sweetest I have ever tasted.